Oxford Read a...

CW00571988

All A...

Ocean Life

Rachel Bladon

Contents

OXFORD
UNIVERSITY PRESS

OXFORD
UNIVERSITY PRESS

Great Clarendon Street, Oxford OX2 6DP

Oxford University Press is a department of the University of Oxford. It furthers the University's objective of excellence in research, scholarship, and education by publishing worldwide in

Oxford New York

Auckland Cape Town Dar es Salaam Hong Kong Karachi Kuala Lumpur Madrid Melbourne Mexico City Nairobi New Delhi Shanghai Taipei Toronto

With offices in

Argentina Austria Brazil Chile Czech Republic France Greece Guatemala Hungary Italy Japan Poland Portugal Singapore South Korea Switzerland Thailand Turkey Ukraine Vietnam

OXFORD and OXFORD ENGLISH are registered trade marks of Oxford University Press in the UK and in certain other countries

ISBN: 978 0 19 464439 6

An Audio CD Pack containing this book and a CD is also available
ISBN: 978 0 19 464479 2
The CD has a choice of American and British English recordings of the complete text.

An accompanying Activity Book is also available
ISBN: 978 0 19 464449 5

Printed in China

This book is printed on paper from certified and well-managed sources.

ACKNOWLEDGEMENTS
Illustrations by: Martin Bustamante/Advocate Art pp5, 6, 26; Alan Rowe pp28, 31, 32, 34, 36, 41, 46, 47; Martin Sanders/ Beehive Illustration pp3, 24; Gary Swift pp5, 7, 14, 16, 19.

The publisher would like to thank the following for their kind permission to reproduce photographs and other copyright material: Alamy Images pp11 (Albatross/David Osborn), 15 (Porcupine fish/Igor Burchenkov), 18 (Polar bear with cubs/Juniors Bildarchiv), 39 (Polar bear with cubs/Juniors Bildarchiv); Ardea p14 (Leafy Seadragon/Auscape); Beach Feature p8 (Shells/Paul Box); Corbis pp11 (Sperm Whale/ Denis Scott), 19 (Penguins/Tim Davies), 39 (Penguins/Tim Davies); Fotolia p13 (Clownfish/Eric Isselée); Getty Images pp9 (Sea Anemone/David Wrobel), 22 (Oil slick on beach/ Ben Osborne); Image Quest Marine p17 (Deep sea angler fish/ NOC/imagequestmarine.com); National Geographic Image Collection pp9 (Forest of Red Mangroves/Norbert Wu/Minden Pictures), 17 (Mangrove Jellyfish/Chris Newbert/Minden Pictures); OUP p3 (crab/Iconotec); PA Photos p21 (Harvesting seaweed/Ed Wray/AP); Photolibrary pp4 (Walruses/Thorsten Milse), 4 (Cook Islands/Charle Avice), 7 (Sea Otter/David Courtenay), 12 (Common Lionfish/Rodger Klein), 20 (Fisherman/James Watt); Photoshot p23 (Green turtle/Oceans-Image); PunchStock p21 (Oyster with pearl/Photographer's Choice); SeaPics.com pp10 (California sea lion), 13 (Yellowfin goatfish), 15 (Octopus), 16 (Hammerhead shark).

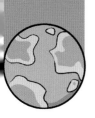

Introduction

A lot of Earth is covered by saltwater oceans. The oceans are home to many types of life, from the smallest plants to the biggest whales.

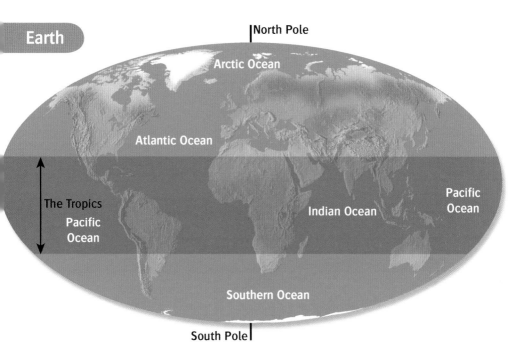

Earth

North Pole

Arctic Ocean

Atlantic Ocean

The Tropics

Pacific Ocean

Pacific Ocean

Indian Ocean

Southern Ocean

South Pole

What do you know about oceans?
Which mammals live in the oceans?
Which animals can you find in icy oceans?

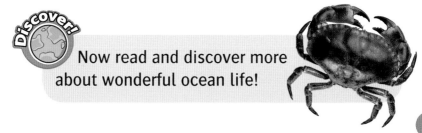

Now read and discover more about wonderful ocean life!

Oceans of the World

There are five oceans, and they cover about 70 percent (%) of Earth. Oceans and their seashores are different all around the world. On the Arctic Ocean and the Southern Ocean there's a lot of ice in winter. In warm tropical oceans you can find colorful coral reefs, where very many plants, fish, and other animals live.

The Arctic

A Tropical Beach

An ocean is always moving because of waves, currents, and tides. When the wind blows over the water, it makes waves. Currents are large amounts of warm or cold water that move around the ocean. An ocean also moves up the seashore and back again two times a day. These movements are called tides.

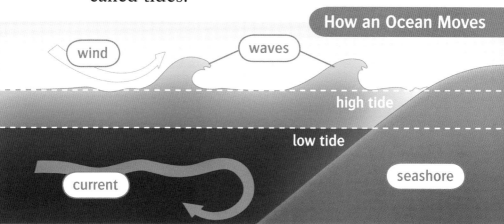

How an Ocean Moves

wind

waves

high tide

low tide

current

seashore

Living in the ocean is very different to living on land. Ocean plants and animals have special ways of breathing, eating, moving, and keeping safe.

Discover!

The blue whale is the biggest animal in the world. It can be more than 30 meters long! It moves well in the ocean because the water holds it up.

→ Go to pages 24–25 for activities.

Who Eats What?

In the ocean there are lots of very small animals and plants called plankton. The plankton live near the top of the ocean because they need sunlight. Small fish eat plankton. Big animals eat the small fish. Then even bigger animals eat them! So plankton are important for almost every ocean animal. This is called a food chain.

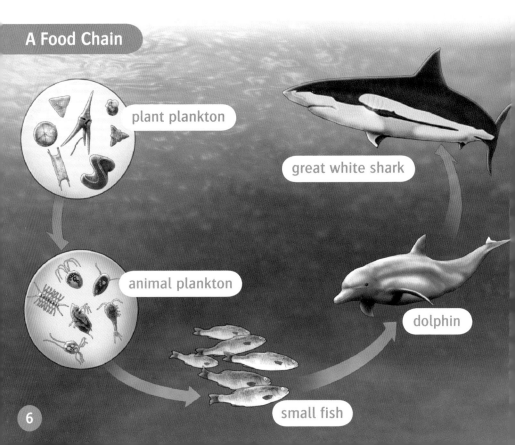

A Food Chain

plant plankton

great white shark

animal plankton

dolphin

small fish

Animals that eat other animals are called predators. The animals that they eat are called prey. Most sharks are predators. Sharks can swim very fast to catch their prey.

Discover! The whale shark is the biggest fish in the world. It's as long as a bus. It has no teeth, so it only eats plankton and small shrimps.

Lots of seaweed called kelp grows near the seashore. The kelp is a safe home for many fish. Sea urchins eat kelp, and sea otters eat a lot of sea urchins. So sea otters help to keep enough kelp in the ocean for the fish to live in.

A Sea Otter Eating a Sea Urchin

Go to pages 26–27 for activities.

The Seashore

There's a lot of ocean life near the seashore because the water here is full of food. Many birds, fish, and shellfish live and feed near the seashore. The seashore is not always a safe place. Big waves can throw animals onto rocks or carry them away. At low tide, animals and plants can easily dry out in the sun.

Limpets are animals that have a special strong foot that holds onto rocks. This keeps them safe from big waves. They also have a hard shell so they don't dry out.

Limpets on a Rock

Mangrove Trees

roots

Most trees can't live in salty ocean water, but mangrove trees grow on the seashore in tropical places. They have special roots so they can live in salt water. Many fish and other animals live under the roots of mangrove trees.

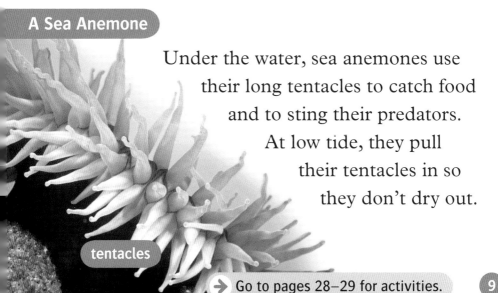

A Sea Anemone

Under the water, sea anemones use their long tentacles to catch food and to sting their predators. At low tide, they pull their tentacles in so they don't dry out.

tentacles

Go to pages 28–29 for activities.

Mammals and Birds

A mammal is an animal that drinks milk from its mother and breathes air. Most mammals, like people and elephants, live on land. Some mammals live in the ocean. Because they feed and move in water, ocean mammals are different from land mammals in many ways.

The sea lion's body has a shape like a fish, so it can swim very fast. It doesn't have front legs, but it has flippers that pull it through the water.

A Sea Lion

flipper

blowhole

Whales are ocean mammals. Like all whales, the sperm whale breathes through a hole on its head called a blowhole. Sperm whales can stay underwater for two hours, and they can dive a long way down into the ocean.

Some birds live, feed, and sleep on the ocean. They catch fish by diving under the water. Some birds only come to the seashore to make nests and to lay eggs.

Discover!

The albatross has bigger wings than any other bird.
The two wings can be more than 3 meters wide!
The albatross can fly up to 1,000 kilometers a day.

➔ Go to pages 30–31 for activities.

5 Coral Reefs

A Lionfish in a Coral Reef

Corals are small animals that make hard covers around themselves. The covers are many different shapes and colors. Coral reefs are places where lots of corals live together. They are beautiful underwater worlds.

Many different plants and animals live on coral reefs. Coral reef fish are very colorful so they are camouflaged – it's not easy to see them near the coral.

Clownfish live near the tentacles of sea anemones. Predators don't come near because the tentacles can sting them. The clownfish are safe because they have a special skin. Predators don't come near lionfish either. The spines of a lionfish can sting a fish and stop it moving, or even kill it.

Small fish called cleaner wrasse work hard on coral reefs. They eat the little plants and animals that live on big fish. Big fish don't eat the cleaner wrasse. They open their mouths so the wrasse can clean inside!

A Cleaner Wrasse at Work

Go to pages 32–33 for activities.

Keeping Safe

Small fish and other animals have to keep safe from predators. Some fish swim together in big groups called shoals. In a shoal, there are more fish to look out for predators. There are also lots of fish to eat. So if a fish is lucky, the predator eats one of the other fish!

The leafy sea dragon is very well camouflaged. When it hides in seaweed, other fish can't see it. Can you see this leafy sea dragon?

A Leafy Sea Dragon

Discover! If a starfish loses an arm, it can grow a new one.

Octopuses camouflage themselves by turning a different color. Can you see this octopus? When an octopus is scared, it can also make a big cloud of black ink. This surprises predators and gives the octopus time to swim away.

When the porcupine fish sees a predator, it drinks lots of water. This makes its body big and round like a ball, and its spines stand up. Predators know that they can't eat it so they don't come near.

➔ Go to pages 34–35 for activities.

7 Catching Prey

eye

nostril

A Hammerhead Shark

Big predators are very good at catching their prey. Sharks can smell and see very well. The hammerhead shark has nostrils and eyes at the ends of its head, so it can see and smell all around.

The electric ray can give other fish an electric shock. This stops them moving, or kills them, so that the ray can eat them.

Discover!

Electric rays make electricity. Some make enough electricity to work a television!

All jellyfish have tentacles that can sting. When a fish swims near a jellyfish, the tentacles sting it many times. The jellyfish can then eat the fish.

The anglerfish lives in deep water, where it's very dark and cold, but it has a small light on its head. When small fish see the light, they think it's something that they can eat. When they swim near, the anglerfish eats them.

→ Go to pages 36–37 for activities.

17

8 Icy Oceans

Large parts of the Arctic Ocean and Southern Ocean have ice on them in winter. There are also big icebergs. In summer, a lot of the ice melts. Then there are little pieces of ice in the oceans, and the icebergs are smaller.

Polar bears live in the Arctic. Most of the year, they live on ice. They catch seals from holes in the ice. They also swim between the ice and icebergs. Polar bears are the biggest type of bear, but their cubs are very, very small when they are born.

A Polar Bear With Cubs

In summer, the Southern Ocean has a lot of plankton. Many dolphins, whales, seals, and birds come there to feed.

Penguins live near the South Pole. They dive into the ocean for fish and other small animals. They have special feathers that keep them warm and dry. Their feathers are so warm that penguins can sometimes get too hot!

Penguins Diving

Discover! A penguin keeps its egg on its feet so it doesn't get cold on the ice.

Go to pages 38–39 for activities.

Farming the Oceans

People started fishing a long time ago, but today, fishermen with big boats can catch a lot of fish. Sometimes we take too many fish from the ocean.

In many parts of the world, people farm fish in the ocean. The fish grow quickly, and they are also easy to catch.

Fishermen at Work

There are other types of farm in the ocean. In some places, farmers grow seaweed. When the seaweed is big enough, farmers collect it and dry it on land. Then they sell it. People eat it, and other farmers put it on their fields.

People use seaweed to make ice cream!

A Seaweed Farm

In the Pacific Ocean, farmers grow pearls. They put pieces of shell inside shellfish called oysters and then they put the oysters on ropes. Hard shiny covers called pearls grow around the shell pieces. Farmers sell pearls for a lot of money.

pearl

oyster

➡ Go to pages 40–41 for activities.

10 Oceans in Danger

There are many dangers for ocean birds and other animals. Big boats carry oil across the oceans. If the oil goes into the water, birds and other animals eat it. It also gets on their skin or feathers. It can kill them.

Dirty water and chemicals from toilets, factories, and farms also go into the oceans. They can kill plants, fish, and other animals. People leave things on the beach, too, and sometimes these things can hurt animals. Sea turtles eat plastic bags because when they are in the water they look like jellyfish.

Sometimes, big fishing nets catch dolphins, sea turtles, seals, and birds. Coral reefs are not safe either because they need clean water. Boats can break them, too.

So now we need to keep the ocean clean and safe. There are new rules so people can't take too many fish from the ocean. There are also new types of fishing net. Big animals can swim out of these nets. Now there are also some marine parks – special places where the ocean is always clean and safe.

A Sea Turtle, Great Barrier Reef Marine Park

Go to pages 42–43 for activities.

1 Oceans of the World

← Read pages 4–5.

1 Write the oceans.

~~Arctic~~ Atlantic Indian
Pacific Southern

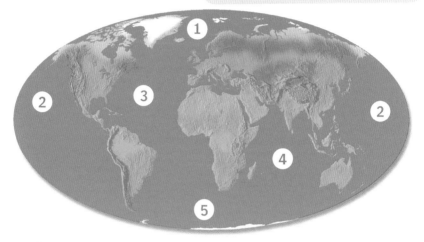

1 _Arctic Ocean_   4 _____

2 _____   5 _____

3 _____

2 Complete the sentences.

70 30 two
~~five~~ two

1 There are _five_ oceans.

2 The oceans cover about _____ % of Earth.

3 There are _____ high and low tides every day.

4 The blue whale can be more than _____
meters long.

5 Earth has _____ Poles.

3 Circle the correct words.

1 A lot of Earth is covered by **land** / **ocean**.

2 In the **Pacific** / **Arctic** Ocean there is ice in winter.

3 Tropical oceans are **colder** / **warmer** than the Arctic.

4 In tropical oceans you can find colorful **ice** / **coral reefs**.

5 When the wind blows over the water, it makes **tides** / **waves**.

6 The blue whale is the **smallest** / **biggest** animal in the world.

7 The **air** / **water** holds up the blue whale.

4 Complete the puzzle.

1 the biggest animal in the world

2 the ocean around the North Pole

3 the ocean around the South Pole

4 large amounts of warm or cold water that move around the ocean

5 the movements of the ocean going up and down the seashore

1 ↓
b
l
4 → u
e
w
h
a
l
e

2 ↓

3 ↓

5 →

② Who Eats What?

← Read pages 6–7.

1 Write the words.

animal plankton   great white shark
small fish   ~~plant plankton~~   dolphin

1 _plant plankton_
2 _____
3 _____
4 _____
5 _____

2 Match. Then write the sentences.

Dolphins eat   dolphins.
Great white sharks eat sea urchins.
Whale sharks eat   small fish.
Sea otters eat   plankton.

1 _Dolphins eat small fish._
2 _____
3 _____
4 _____

3 Answer the questions.

1 What are plankton?

They are very small animals and plants.

2 Why do they live near the top of the ocean?

_____

3 What is a predator?

_____

4 What is the biggest fish in the world?

_____

5 What is kelp?

_____

4 Draw and write about a food chain.

_____

_____

_____

_____

_____

_____

_____

_____

3 The Seashore

← Read pages 8–9.

mangrove trees   shellfish
sea anemones   limpets

1 Write the words.

1 _____

2 _____

3 _____

4 _____

2 Complete the sentences.

tentacles   salt   animals   dry out
rocks   low tide   shell   seashore

1 Many _____ live near the _____ because the water is full of food.

2 Animals and plants can dry out at _____.

3 Limpets hold onto _____ with a special strong foot.

4 Limpets have a hard _____ so they don't dry out.

5 Mangrove trees have special roots so they can live in _____ water.

6 Sea anemones pull their _____ in so they don't _____.

3 Complete the chart.

sea anemones   sharks   animal plankton
kelp   limpets   sea urchins   mangrove trees
plant plankton   shrimps   sea otters   whales

Ocean Animals		Ocean Plants
sea anemones	_____	_____
_____	_____	_____
_____	_____	_____
_____	_____	

4 What is it? Write the answers.

a limpet   a sea anemone   a shark
a mangrove tree   plankton

1 It has a strong foot and a hard shell. _a limpet_

2 It has long tentacles for catching food. _____

3 Many fish and other animals live under its special roots. _____

4 It can swim very fast. _____

5 They are very small animals and plants. _____

4 Mammals and Birds

← Read pages 10–11.

1 Circle the correct words.

1 A mammal drinks **water** / **milk** from its mother.

2 The sea lion has **front legs** / **flippers**.

3 The sperm whale breathes through its **mouth** / **blowhole**.

4 It can stay underwater for **two hours** / **twenty minutes**.

5 Some ocean birds only come to the seashore to lay **nests** / **eggs**.

6 The albatross has **bigger wings** / **a longer tail** than any other bird.

2 Complete the diagram.

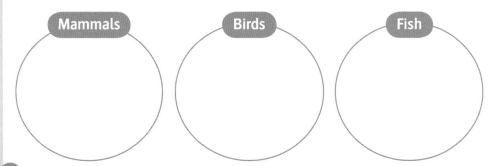

albatross   sea lion   sperm whale
blue whale   shark   dolphin

Mammals   Birds   Fish

3 Write about another ocean animal.

Name:	dolphin 	
Mammal, fish or bird?	mammal	
Eats:	fish and squid	
Lives:	all over the world	
Description:	gray color it has a fish shape	
Interesting facts:	it can see and hear very well it makes loud noises to help it move around safely	

⑤ Coral Reefs

← Read pages 12–13.

cleaner wrasse   sea anemone
sea urchin   shark
lionfish   clownfish

1 Write the words.

1 _____

2 _____

3 _____

4 _____

5 _____

6 _____

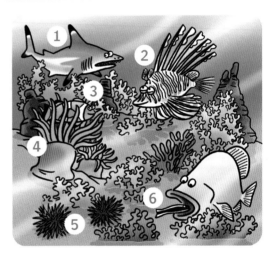

2 Match.

1 They are small animals with hard covers.

2 They sting predators with their tentacles.

3 They live near the tentacles of sea anemones.

4 They have spines that can sting.

5 They clean other fish.

lionfish

corals

cleaner wrasse

clownfish

sea anemones

3 **Write _true_ or _false_.**

1 Corals are all the same shape. _false_

2 There are not many plants or animals on
coral reefs. _____

3 It is hard to see animals that are
camouflaged. _____

4 Clownfish live near the tentacles of sea
anemones to keep safe from predators. _____

5 Lionfish have tentacles that sting fish. _____

6 Fish eat cleaner wrasse when they are
cleaning their mouths. _____

4 **Complete the sentences.**

skin   kill   mouths   camouflaged   colors

1 Corals have covers that are many different
shapes and _____ .

2 Coral reef fish are very colorful so they are
well _____ .

3 Sea anemones don't sting clownfish because
they have a special _____ .

4 If a lionfish stings a fish it can _____ it.

5 Fish open their _____ when cleaner wrasse
clean inside.

6 Keeping Safe

← Read pages 14–15.

leafy sea dragon   octopus
porcupine fish   starfish
shoal of fish   seaweed

1 Write the words.

1 _____   2 _____   3 _____

4 _____   5 _____   6 _____

2 Match.

To keep safe ...

1 It grows a new arm.
2 It turns a different shape so that nothing can eat it.
3 It makes a cloud of black ink.
4 It hides in seaweed.
5 They swim together in big groups.
6 It turns a different color.

an octopus

an octopus

a porcupine fish

a starfish

a leafy sea dragon

a shoal of fish

3 Answer the questions.

1 What are big groups of fish called?

_____

2 What does the leafy sea dragon look like?

_____

3 How do octopuses camouflage themselves?

_____

4 What do octopuses do when they are scared?

_____

5 What does the porcupine fish do when it sees
a predator?

_____

6 What happens to a porcupine fish's body?

_____

4 Draw and write about an ocean animal.

This ocean animal is called

_____.

When it sees a predator, it

_____.

It does this to _____

_____.

7 Catching Prey

← Read pages 16–17.

jellyfish   teeth   tentacles
shark   head   light
nostril   anglerfish   eye

1 Write the words.

1 _____   4 _____   7 _____

2 _____   5 _____   8 _____

3 _____   6 _____   9 _____

2 Circle the correct words.

1 The animals that big animals eat are called their **prey** / **predators**.

2 The hammerhead shark has nostrils and eyes at the ends of its **head** / **body**.

3 Some electric rays make enough electricity to work a **television** / **train**.

4 The jellyfish catches its prey with **tentacles** / **spines**.

5 The anglerfish lives in **warm** / **dark** water.

6 The anglerfish has a light on its **head** / **teeth**.

3 **Complete the sentences. Then match.**

stings   smell   light   shock

1 It gives fish an electric _____ . ☐ anglerfish

2 It can see and _____ all around. ☐ jellyfish

3 It _____ fish with its tentacles. [1] electric ray

4 It has a _____ on its head so ☐ hammerhead
   other fish swim near.   shark

4 **Draw and write about two ocean predators.**

This ocean predator is

called _____ .

It is special because

_____ .

To catch prey, it _____

_____ .

_____

_____

_____

_____

_____

_____

8 Icy Oceans

← Read pages 18–19.

1 Find and write the animals.

p	o	l	a	r	b	e	a	r
e	f	d	e	h	i	d	w	g
n	f	k	o	j	r	l	z	r
g	s	e	a	l	d	i	c	a
u	a	e	o	y	p	w	e	l
i	j	d	u	i	c	h	p	g
n	a	e	e	k	o	a	i	h
c	s	b	a	u	m	l	v	n
b	n	t	a	i	i	e	x	q

1 bird
2 _____
3 _____
4 _____
5 _____
6 _____

2 Circle the correct words.

1 There is **a lot of** / **not much** ice on the Arctic and Southern Oceans in winter.

2 The icebergs are smaller in **summer** / **winter**.

3 Polar bears are the **biggest** / **smallest** type of bear, but their cubs are very **big** / **small**.

4 Many animals come to the Southern Ocean in summer because there is a lot of **ice** / **food**.

5 Penguins live near the **South** / **North** Pole.

6 A penguin keeps its egg on its **feet** / **feathers**.

3 Write about polar bears and penguins.

Three things that I read about
polar bears on page 18:

1 _____

2 _____

3 _____

Another thing that I know about polar bears:

_____

Three things that I read about
penguins on page 19:

1 _____

2 _____

3 _____

Another thing that I know about penguins:

_____

9 Farming the Oceans

← Read pages 20–21.

1 Complete the puzzle.

1 Fishermen with big boats catch a lot of these.

2 Farmers can sell these for a lot of money.

3 This is cold and can have seaweed in it.

4 Some farmers put this on their fields.

5 Farmers put these on ropes.

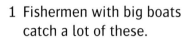

2 Write *true* or *false*.

1 Today, people do not catch a lot of fish in the ocean. _____

2 It is easy to catch fish in ocean farms. _____

3 Fish in ocean farms grow very slowly. _____

4 You can't eat seaweed. _____

5 Pearls start as pieces of shell. _____

6 People buy pearls for a lot of money. _____

3 Complete the sentences. Then write the numbers.

shell   pearls   money   ~~oysters~~   ropes

1 The farmer collects _oysters._

2 The farmer puts pieces of _____ inside.

3 The farmer puts the oysters on _____ .

4 _____ grow.

5 The farmer sells the pearls for a lot of _____ .

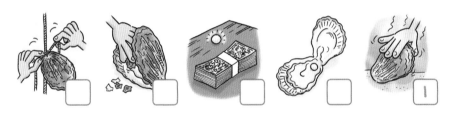

collects   put   sells   dries   grows

6 The seaweed _____ in the ocean.

7 The farmer _____ the seaweed.

8 The farmer _____ the seaweed on land.

9 Then the farmer _____ it.

10 Other farmers _____ seaweed on their fields.

10 Oceans in Danger

← Read pages 22–23.

1 Complete the sentences.

marine parks   plastic bags   oil
fishing nets   chemicals

1 Sometimes _____ from big boats goes into the ocean.

2 Dirty water and _____ from toilets, factories, and farms go into the ocean.

3 Sea turtles think _____ are jellyfish.

4 Sometimes fishermen catch dolphins, sea turtles, seals, and birds in their _____ .

5 _____ are special places where the ocean is always clean and safe.

2 Answer the questions.

1 Why is oil a problem?

_____

2 Why are plastic bags dangerous?

_____

3 What is the problem with big fishing nets?

_____

3 Complete the chart.

boats break coral reefs   dirty water and chemicals
big nets catch animals   fishermen take too many fish
people leave things on beaches   oil

Dangers for the Ocean		
Pollution	**Fishing**	**Damage**
_____	_____	_____
_____	_____	_____
_____	_____	_____
_____	_____	_____

4 Write the solutions.

1 Problem: Big boats catch a lot of fish.

Solution: There are new rules so people can't take too many fish from the ocean.

2 Problem: Big fishing nets catch dolphins, sea turtles, seals, and birds.

Solution: _____

3 Problem: Dirty water, oil, and chemicals go into the ocean.

Solution: _____

Oceans in Danger

1 Think of some dangers for ocean life in or near your country. Write notes.

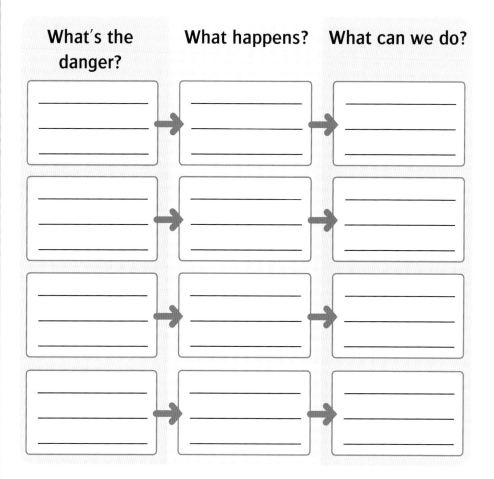

What's the danger?	What happens?	What can we do?

2 Make a poster. Write about oceans in danger and add pictures.

3 Display your poster.

A Food Chain

1 Write the names of ocean life in or near your country.

Mammals	Birds	Fish	Other Animals
_____	_____	_____	_____
_____	_____	_____	_____
_____	_____	_____	_____
_____	_____	_____	_____
_____	_____	_____	_____

2 Write the names of four animals to make a food chain.

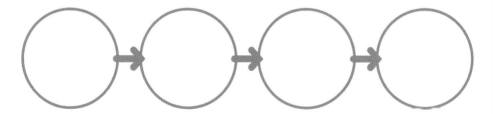

3 Make a food chain poster. Draw pictures and write about your food chain.

4 Display your food chain poster.

Picture Dictionary

 breathe

 chemicals

 coral reef

 cover

 danger

 deep

 dirty

 dive

 dry out

 electric shock

 electricity

 feather

 fishing net

 grow

 hide

 hole

 hurt

 ice

 iceberg

 ink

kill

lay eggs

melt

nest

nostril

oil

plastic bag

rules

salt

seal

seaweed

shell

shellfish

shrimp

skin

smell

spine

sting

top

waves

Oxford Read and Discover

Series Editor: Hazel Geatches • CLIL Adviser: John Clegg

Oxford Read and Discover graded readers are at four levels, from 3 to 6, suitable for students from age 8 and older. They cover many topics within three subject areas, and can support English across the curriculum, or Content and Language Integrated Learning (CLIL).

Available for each reader:
• Audio CD Pack (book & audio CD)
• Activity Book

For Teacher's Notes & CLIL Guidance go to
www.oup.com/elt/teacher/readanddiscover

Subject Area / Level	The World of Science & Technology	The Natural World	The World of Arts & Social Studies
3 600 headwords	• How We Make Products • Sound and Music • Super Structures • Your Five Senses	• Amazing Minibeasts • Animals in the Air • Life in Rainforests • Wonderful Water	• Festivals Around the World • Free Time Around the World
4 750 headwords	• All About Plants • How to Stay Healthy • Machines Then and Now • Why We Recycle	• All About Desert Life • All About Ocean Life • Animals at Night • Incredible Earth	• Animals in Art • Wonders of the Past
5 900 headwords	• Materials to Products • Medicine Then and Now • Transportation Then and Now • Wild Weather	• All About Islands • Animal Life Cycles • Exploring Our World • Great Migrations	• Homes Around the World • Our World in Art
6 1,050 headwords	• Cells and Microbes • Clothes Then and Now • Incredible Energy • Your Amazing Body	• All About Space • Caring for Our Planet • Earth Then and Now • Wonderful Ecosystems	• Helping Around the World • Food Around the World

For younger students, **Dolphin Readers** Levels Starter, 1, and 2 are available.